Hydroponics Bi'
Dun

The Ultimate Guide on How to design an inexpensive structure for growing various plants in water

Oprah Kirby

ISBN: 978-1-63750-066-8

Table of Contents

Introduction

Do you love gardening and would like to grow your fruits, vegetables, and herbs, but don't have a garden or enough space to plant? Need not worry. A hydroponic growing system gives you the ability to grow healthy plants faster anywhere.

No soil or sunlight? No problem, hydroponics got you covered. Is water scarce? Hydroponic systems are enclosed, and evaporation is not allowed, making water loss from the system impossible.

Are you exhausted about the time and money spent on buying genetically modified and chemically treated products from the store? Would you like to learn how to set up your own aquaponic garden where healthy produce can be cultivated?

Even if you have been involved in soil gardening before, and would like to explore a different and faster gardening technique; the instructions in this accessible guide will help you become an expert in growing plants hydroponically, and also effectively managing your plants;

and you don't have to be a commercial farmer to make this work for you! Simply add essential nutrients into a water-based solution, and circulate it through a network of pipes and vessels to the plant roots. It's that simple!

Oprah Kirby gives us the blueprint with proven strategies and DIY steps on how to grow vegetables, fruits, and herbs successfully, how to create efficient hydroponic systems, and maintenance techniques for vibrant-looking and healthy plants.

Also included are:

- The beginners' guide to hydroponics

- Good starter plants that can be grown using hydroponics

- Maintenance and growing instructions to put pests under control and prevent plant diseases.

- Simple DIY hydroponic systems (with equipment guide) that can be made in your home

- Selecting the best Ventilation and Light source for

your plant (natural and artificial lighting techniques)

- How to choose the best nutrient solution for your hydroponic system and plant

- Major systems and the plants they best suit.

- Making nutrient solutions at home, with recipes

- How to assemble and build a homemade hydroponic system

These are all presented with clear explanations to aid understanding.

Chapter 1

What is Hydroponics?

Hydroponics is the growing of vegetation/plant in a liquid nutritional solution with or without the utilization of artificial media. Popular mediums include expanded clay, coir, perlite, vermiculite, brick shards, polystyrene packaging, and solid wood fiber. Hydroponics has been acknowledged as a practical approach to producing vegetables (tomatoes, leafy greens, lettuce, cucumbers, and peppers) as well as ornamental plants such as natural herbs, roses, freesia, and foliage plant. Because of the ban on methyl bromide in soil, the demand for hydroponically grown crops/produce has quickly increased within the last few years.

Hydroponics is a great choice for all kinds of growers. It really is a fantastic choice since it provides you the capability to meticulously control the factors that impact how well your vegetation grows. A fine-tuned hydroponic system can simply surpass a soil-based system in plant quality and amount of produce yielded.

If you wish to grow the largest, juiciest, yummiest plant life you can possibly imagine, then hydroponics is a good choice for you. It could seem intimidating initially with all the current equipment and work included, but it'll all seem not difficult once you get the hang of the basics. Start small, keep it simple, and your hydroponic system won't stop to amaze!

Background

The word hydroponics originates from two Greek words 'hydro' meaning water and 'ponos' meaning labor. This term was first used in 1929 by Dr. Gericke, a California teacher who began to build up what previously has been a laboratory technique into a commercial method of growing vegetation. The U.S. Army used hydroponic culture to grow fresh food for soldiers stationed on infertile Pacific islands during World War II. From the 1950s, there have been practical commercial farms in the US, European countries, Africa and Asia.

The hanging Gardens of Babylon as well as the Floating Gardens of China are two of the earlier types of hydroponics. Researchers started tinkering with soil less gardening around 1950. Since that time other countries, such as Holland, Germany, and Australia have used hydroponics for crop creation with amazing results.

In India, Hydroponics started in 1946 by a British scientist, W. J. Shalto Duglas, and he founded a lab in Kalimpong area, Western Bengal. With time, Hydroponics farms were developed in Abu Dhabi, Az, Belgium, California, Denmark, German, Holland, Iran, Italy, Japan, Russian Federation, and other countries. During the 1980s, many automated and computerized hydroponics farms were set up around the world. Home hydroponics kits became popular during 1990s.

Chapter 2

The Beginners' Guide

At the most fundamental level, hydroponics is a way of growing vegetation in a water and nutrient solution without garden soil. Rather than the earth providing the plant life sustenance, the macro and micronutrients essential for vegetation are added yourself through mixtures that may be purchased online or at one of the numerous hydroponic retailers. The technique allows the root base to have an immediate connection with the nutrition and air for a far more effective and frequently speedier growing experience.

There are a number of hydroponic systems that test out the many ways plants can absorb water through their roots. Hydroponic systems come in different sizes and shapes, from desktop aeroponic plant gardens to large commercial hydroponic businesses.

The substrates that keep carefully the roots set up vary

widely as well, from sand and pebbles to coconut shells and Rockwool.

Basic hydroponic systems don't need to be complicated, though; you can arrange one up in your house with just a little creativeness (or a small amount of money to buy a pre-made system). Hydroponics is specially great for metropolitan homesteaders with the absence of large yards, or flower aficionados seeking to green up their winter blues with some creative indoor horticulture.

Setting up a Hydroponic system

You can test out a few of the more technical methods as you grow convenient with the fundamentals. However, the easiest hydroponic way for beginners is Deep Water Culture or DWC. In this technique, the plant life roots are suspended in the water-nutrient solution and oxygenated via an external source.

A starter hydroponic package that uses this technique can get you started, or just use a 20-gallon aquarium container or plastic material bin, an aquarium pump, some seedlings and styrofoam with openings for the seedlings to grow in.

The spacing for the openings in the styrofoam depends on the seed; lettuce will require about 8inches between plantings to provide the heads with sufficient space to develop.

You'll also need a hydroponic nutrient combination, which acts as a sort of fertilizer for your water-borne vegetation.

The requisite ratio of water to nutrients will be written in the nutrients' instructions. More water and nutrient blend should be added every couple of weeks as the plant life lap up the Nutrient solution. However, in places where water is hard, the sodium chloride used to soften water could harm some vegetation.

Due to the confluence of water, nutrition, and light; hydroponic systems can be hotbeds for algae. Generally, algae won't hurt your plant life, but it could be disquieting.

It's more aesthetic than any other thing. The ultimate way to prevent algae from growing is to ensure water is always in darkness. You could grow the vegetation within an opaque bottomed bin, or cover the container with black building paper up to the waterline.

The logistics of hydroponics can appear intimidating for homesteaders. However, the experts all concur that the ultimate way to get started doing hydroponics is merely to check it out for yourself and start.

An essential thing to do is just do it, and also have fun in the process.

Factors to consider when choosing Hydroponic techniques

1. Space and other available resources

2. Expected productivity

3. Option of suitable growing medium

4. Expected quality of the produce, that is, color, appearance, free from pesticides, etc.

Starter Plants

Some vegetation that works nicely for beginners just learning the fundamentals of hydroponic gardening include the following:

- Greens vegetables such as lettuce, spinach, Swiss chard, and kale

- Natural herbs such as basil, parsley, oregano, cilantro and mint

- Tomatoes

- Strawberries

- Hot Peppers

Chapter 3

Advantages of hydroponics?

The most significant benefit of a hydroponic system over a soil-based garden is control. You can provide the vegetation whatever it wants. Water and nutrition can be utilized more effectively because you have the knowledge of what the plants need, and you simply source it to them.

Once you have a hydroponic system, your garden is no more at the whims of the weather. Mother Earth may be happy, and sometimes not. Using an inside hydroponic system, you understand steps to make the plant life happy always.

When done correctly, hydroponic gardening also grows vegetation faster and more resource-efficiently. Bringing up plants hydroponically uses about 90 percent less water than growing them on a soil medium.

Furthermore, soil-borne pathogens are a common reason behind the death of most plants. Another benefit is that since there is no soil, you have actually removed one of the primary sources of disease problems. Most of the diseases that affect vegetation are fungi and bacteria that reside in the soil.

Having access to a view of the plant's root results in easier troubleshooting. One of the benefits of hydroponics is that you will get an opportunity to see what the roots appear to be. White roots are healthy, but if you see black or brownish development/growth on the root, maybe it's some kind of bacteria indicating that you'll require to change the water or replace the hydroponic system entirely.

Hydroponics is proved to have several advantages over soil gardening. The development rate and yield of a hydroponic plant is 30-50% faster when compared to a soil plant, cultivated under the same conditions. The yield of the plant is also higher. Scientists think that there are several known reasons for the extreme variations between hydroponic and ground plants. The excess air in the hydroponic growing mediums really helps to stimulate main growth. Plant life with ample air in the main system also absorb nutrition faster. The nutrition in a hydroponic system is blended with water and delivered directly to the main system. The plant doesn't have to find in the soil for the nutrition that it needs. The nutrients are being sent to the plant several times each day. The hydroponic plant requires hardly any energy to find and breakdown food. The plant then uses this preserved energy to develop faster and also to produce more fruits. Hydroponic plants have fewer issues with insect/bug infestations, funguses and disease. Generally, plants cultivated hydroponically are healthier and happier plants.

Hydroponic gardening offers several benefits to your environment. Hydroponic gardening uses substantially less water than soil gardening, because of the continuous reuse of the nutrient solutions. Because of lack of requirement and necessity, fewer pesticides are applied to hydroponic plants.

Since hydroponic gardening systems use no topsoil, topsoil erosion isn't even a concern. Although, if Agricultural trends continue steadily to erode topsoil and wastewater, hydroponics may soon be our only solution.

Hydroponic systems may also be more expensive to create when compared to a garden in your yard - not only in terms of the infrastructure, but also the price of water and electricity necessary to keep up with the system.

A hydroponic system will also use less water than soil grown plants because the system is enclosed, which leads to less evaporation. Contrary to popular belief, hydroponics is way better for the surroundings since it reduces waste materials and air pollution from soil runoff.

Hydroponics can be an advantage in places where in-ground agriculture or gardening is extremely hard (for example, desert areas or cold climate regions).

Complete control of nutrient content, pH, and growing environment.

Lower water and nutrient costs due to water and nutrient recycling.

Faster growth due to more available oxygen in root area.

Elimination or reduced amount of soil-related insects, fungi and bacteria.

Weeding or cultivation is not required.

Some crops, such as lettuce and strawberries, can be

lifted from the level of the ground to a far greater height for planting, cultivation, and harvesting. Thus giving far better working conditions and therefore lowers labor costs.

Crop rotation/fallowing is not essential.

Transplant shock is reduced.

Disadvantages

Even though a hydroponics system has so many advantages, there are a few disadvantages as well. The most significant factor for many people is that a quality hydroponics system of any size will definitely cost more than its soil counterpart. On the other hand, soil isn't expensive, and also you get what you purchase.

The benefit of control may also be a disadvantage. Hydroponic systems require more maintenance and tend to be less forgiving. If you leave things to chance, you can overdose your plants with nutrients or starve it.

A large scale hydroponics system may take lots of time to create if you aren't an experienced grower. Plus, controlling your hydroponics system will need lots of time as well. You will need to monitor and balance your pH and nutritional levels daily.

The most considerable risk of a hydroponics system is that something like a pump failure can kill off your plants within hours depending on the size of your system. They are able to die quickly because the growing medium can't store water like soil can; therefore, the plants are reliant on a fresh supply of water.

Operational and initial expenses of Hydroponics are higher than soil culture.

Skill and knowledge are necessary for proper operation.

Some diseases like *Verticillium* and *Fusarium* spread very fast through the system. However, varieties resistant to the disease conditions mentioned above have been bred.

What's Growing medium?

Growing medium is the materials where the roots of the plant are growing. This addresses a vast variety of chemicals such as Rockwool, perlite, vermiculite, coconut fiber, gravel, fine sand and so many more. The growing medium is an inert material that doesn't provide any nourishment to the plant life. All the nutrition originates from the nutrient solution (water and fertilizer mixed). You can, therefore, easily control everything the vegetation receives. The strength and pH of the nutritional solution are simple to adjust, so the plant receives the ideal amount of food. The watering/feeding cycles can be managed by a cheap timer, so the vegetation get watered on routine, as needed.

The goal of Growing Mediums

The goal of a growing medium is to aerate and support the root system of the plant and also to channel water and nutrients. Different growing media work well in various types of hydroponic systems. A speedy draining medium, such as Hydrocorn or extended shale, is effective within an ebb and flow type system. Hydrocorn is a light extended clay aggregate. It really is a light, airy kind of growing medium that allows a lot of air to permeate the plant's root system. Both types can be reused, even though shale has more tendency to breakdown and might not last so long as the Hydrocorn. These grow rocks are extremely stable and hardly ever impact the pH of the nutritional solution.

Rockwool is becoming an exceptionally popular growing medium. Rockwool was originally used in construction as insulation. There is currently a horticultural grade of Rockwool. Unlike the insulation grade, horticultural Rockwool is pressed into growing cubes and blocks. It really is created from volcanic rock and limestone. These components are melted at temps of 2500 degrees and higher. The molten solution is poured over a rotating cylinder, much like just how cotton candy is manufactured, then pressed into identical sheets, blocks or cubes. Since Rockwool keeps 10-14 times as much water as the soil and retains 20 percent air, it could be used in virtually any hydroponic system. The gardener must be cautious of the pH; since Rockwool has a pH of 7.8, it can boost the pH of the nutrient solution. Rockwool can't be used indefinitely & most gardeners only get one use per cube. Additionally, it is popular for propagation.

Other widely used growing mediums are perlite, vermiculite, and various grades of sand. These three mediums are stable and rarely affect the pH of the nutritional solution. Although, they have a tendency to keep too much moisture and should be used with plant life that are tolerant to these conditions. Perlite, vermiculite and sands are extremely inexpensive options, and work charitably in wick systems, although they aren't the very best growing mediums.

Other points you should know about growing system

Hydroponic systems can either be liquid or aggregate.

Liquid systems do not have any assisting medium for the place root base; whereas, aggregate systems have a good medium of support. Hydroponic systems are further categorized as open (after the nutrient solution is sent to the plant roots, it is not reused) or closed (surplus solution is recovered, replenished, and recycled).

Liquid Hydroponic System:

They are closed systems.

- Nutrient Film Technique (NFT): Vegetation are positioned in a polyethylene pipe that has slits cut in the plastic for the roots to be inserted. Nutrient solution is pumped through this tube.

- Floating Hydroponics: Plants are grown on the floating raft of expanded plastic.

- Aeroponics: Plant roots remain suspended within an enclosed growing chamber, where these are sprayed with a mist of nutrient solution at short intervals, usually every short while.

Aggregate Hydroponic System:

Open system:

- Rockwool Culture: It's the most widely medium in hydroponics. Rockwool is ground-up basalt rock and roll that is warmed then spun into threads making wool. It's very light and it is most times sold in cubes. Rockwool can take water and retain sufficient air space (at least 18 percent) to market ideal root growth.

- Sand Culture

  Closed system:

- Gravel

- NFT and Rockwool: Plants are situated on small rockwool slabs situated in channels made up of recycled nutritional solution.

These systems are further classified into:

1. Passive system

2. Active system

1. Passive systems make use of a wick and growing media

with high capillary action. This allows water to be attracted to the plant roots. The Wick System is undoubtedly the most straightforward kind of hydroponic system

2. Active systems work by passing a nutrient solution actively over the plant roots.

For instance: Water Culture System is the easiest and simplest of all active hydroponic systems. The material that takes hold of the vegetation is usually manufactured from Styrofoam and floats on the nutritional solution. An air pump produces air to the air stone that in turn makes the nutritional solution bubble and gives air to the plant roots.

The Ebb and Stream System functions by temporarily flooding the grow tray with nutrient solution and after this, draining the solution back to the tank. This step is done normally with a submerged pump that is linked to a timer. The timer is set to turn on several times per day, with respect to the size and kind of vegetation, temperature, humidity, and the kind of growing medium used.

Drip systems are the most widely utilized hydroponic system on earth. A timer is controlling a submersed pump. The timer switches the pump on, and nutritional solution is dripped on the root of each plant by a little drip line.

NFT Systems have a continuous flow of nutritional solution, so no timer is necessary for the submersible pump.

The Aeroponic System is the most high-tech kind of hydroponics. The nutritional pump is controlled by a timer just like other kinds of hydroponic systems, except the aeroponic system requires a brief routine timer that operates the pump for a couple of seconds every short while.

Nutrients

A lot of the principles that apply to soil fertilizers also apply to hydroponic fertilizers or nutrient solutions. A hydroponic nutritional solution consists of all the elements that the plant normally would get from the soil. These nutrients can be bought at a hydroponic supply store. They are most times highly concentrated, using 2 to 4 teaspoons per gallon of drinking water. They come in water mixes or powdery mixes, usually with at least two different storage containers, one for growth and the other for bloom. The liquid is somewhat more costly but easy and simple to use. They dissolve quickly and completely into the tank and frequently have an extra pH buffer. The powdery types are inexpensive and need a bit more attention. They have to be combined and mixed thoroughly and frequently don't dissolve completely into the tank. Most don't have a pH buffer.

Chapter 4
Hydroponic Systems

Hydroponic systems are characterized as active or passive. An active hydroponic system actively moves the nutritional solution, usually with a pump. Passive hydroponic systems rely on the capillary action of the growing medium or a wick. The nutrient solution is absorbed by the medium or the wick, and transferred along to the roots. Passive systems are usually too wet and don't supply enough oxygen to the root system for ideal growth rates.

Hydroponic systems may also be characterized as recovery or non-recovery. Recovery systems or recirculating systems reuse the nutritional solution. Non-recovery means precisely what it says. The nutritional solution is applied to the growing medium and not recovered.

Continuous Drip

The Continuous Drip system can be an active recovery or non-recovery type of system. This technique runs on the submersible pump in a tank with supply lines heading to each plant. With drip emitter for each of the plants, the gardener can adjust the quantity of solution per plant. A drip tray under each row of plants, sending the solution back to the tank, can easily make this system an active recovery type. In the first times of hydroponics, the excess solution was leached out into the ground. Continuous Drip systems tend to be used in combination with Rockwool. Although, any growing medium can be used with this technique, because of the modification/adjustment feature on each individual drip emitter.

The Wick System

The wick system is a passive non-recovery type hydroponic system. It uses no pump and does not have any moving parts. The nutrients are stored in the tank and moved into the root system by capillary action often utilizing a candle or lantern wick. In simpler words, the nutritional solution travels up the wick and into the root system of the plant. Wick systems often use sand or perlite, vermiculite blend, and a growing medium. The wick system is simple and cheap to set-up and keeps maintaining. Although, it will keep the growing medium to be wet, which doesn't enable the ideal amount of oxygen in the root system. The wick system is not the most effective way to garden hydroponically.

Deepwater Culture System

Deepwater CultureDeepwater Culture (DWC), also called the tank method, is by far the easiest way for growing plants with hydroponics. Inside a Deepwater Culture hydroponic system, the root base is suspended in a nutritional solution. An aquarium air pump oxygenates the nutritional solution; this keeps the roots of the plants from drowning. Be sure you prevent light from penetrating the system, as this may cause algae to grow. This will wreak havoc on the system.

The principal benefit of utilizing a Deepwater Culture system is that there will be no drip or spray emitters to clog. This makes DWC a great and excellent choice for organic hydroponics, as hydroponics systems that use organic nutrition are more susceptible to clogs.

The Ebb and Flow System

The Ebb and Flow hydroponic system can be an active recovery type system. The Ebb and Flow utilizes the submersible pump in the tank/reservoir, and the plants are in the upper tray. They focus on a simple flood and drain theory. The tank holds the nutritional solution and the pump. When the pump turns on, the nutrient solution is pumped up to the upper tray and sent to the root system of the plant. The pump should be turned on for approximately 20 to 30 minutes, which is known as a flood cycle. After the water has already reached a set level, an overflow tube/pipe or fitting allows the nutritional solution to drain back into the tank/reservoir. The pump remains on for the whole flood cycle. Just after the flood cycle, the nutrient solution gradually drains back into the tank through the pump.

During the Flood pattern, oxygen poor air is forced from the underlying system by the upward moving nutrient solution. As the nutritional solution drains back to the reservoir, air rich air is pulled in to the growing medium. This enables the roots to have sufficient oxygen to increase their nutrient consumption. Rockwool and grow rocks are mostly used growing mediums in Ebb and Flow type systems. The Ebb and Circulation is zero-maintenance (or low maintenance), yet effective kind of hydroponic gardening.

Nutrient Film Technique

The Nutrient Film Technique or NFT system can be an active recovery type of hydroponic system. Again, using submersible pumps and reusing nutritional solutions. The NFT makes use of a tank with a submersible pump that pushes the nutritional solution into a grow-tube where the root base is suspended. The grow-tube is at a slightly downward angle therefore the nutritional solution runs over the roots and back to the tank. The nutritional solution flows on the roots for up to 24 hours per day.

Oxygen is necessary in the grow-tube, so capillary matting or air stones must be used. The vegetation is organized and held up with a support collar or a grow-basket, and no growing medium should be used. The NFT system is quite effective. Although, many beginner hydroponic growers find it hard to fine-tune. It may also be very unforgiving, without growing medium to hold any moisture, any prolonged interruption in the nutritional circulation can cause the roots to dry and the vegetation to suffer and perhaps die.

Aeroponics System

Aeroponics system is a method in hydroponics where the roots of a plant are misted with nutritional solution while suspended in the air. We have two primary approaches to get the solution is to the uncovered root. The first method entails a fine spray nozzle to mist the roots. The other method uses what's called a pond fogger. If you opt to use a pond fogger then be sure you use a Teflon coated disc, as this will certainly reduce the amount of maintenance required.

You might have heard about the AeroGarden, which really is a commercialized aeroponics system. The AeroGarden is a great entryway to aeroponics. It's a turn-key system that will require little setup. In addition, it includes great support and materials to get you started.

Chapter 5

Purchasing a System or Building a System

This is actually the most asked question associated with hydroponics. Do I buy one or build one? This writer recommends a small amount of both. When you have an engineer's mind and imagine building your own hydroponic system, buy one first! Getting a cheap system will help you to get your feet wet and present you a much better knowledge of how hydroponics works. The practical experience will probably be worth the expense of the system, and you'll likely be able to reuse the parts in this system when you set out to build your own.

If you would prefer to get directly into building your own, research your facts. Get every information you can and do not rely on just a single source. This is a constantly changing industry, and there are numerous books still on the shelves that are already outdated. Building your own system can be quite rewarding or extremely frustrating. It's mainly trial and error so, show patience.

Hydroponic gardening is the wave of the future. It is being studied in classrooms around the United States, local horticultural societies, and government funded research at major universities and NASA. Additionally, it is gradually becoming a popular hobby. Hydroponics is fun, exciting and easy to be involved in.

Types of Hydroponic Systems

The cool thing about hydroponics is that we now have many types of hydroponics systems available. Among the better hydroponic systems on the marketplace combine different kinds of hydroponics into one cross hydroponic system. Hydroponics is exclusive for the reason that there are multiple techniques you may use to get the nutrient means to fix your plants.

Useful Tips

- We recommend changing the nutritional solution in your tank every 2-3 weeks.

- Keep the water temperature in your reservoir between 65 and 75 degrees. You are able to maintain the water temperature by utilizing a water heater or a drinking water chiller.

- An air pump with an air stone connected by versatile tubing can assist in circulation and keep your nutritional solution oxygenated.

- If your plant doesn't look healthy, either discolored or distorted, then the very first thing you should check and adjust the pH. If you discover that the pH is not the problem then flush the system with a solution like Clearex.

- We recommend following a feeding cycle provided by the product manufacturer of your nutrients..

- Clean, flush and sterilize your complete system once you finish a growing cycle/routine. Drain your tank and remove any particles, then run your complete system for approximately one day with a mix of non-chlorine bleach and water. Use 1/8th of the glass of non-chlorine bleach for each gallon of drinking water. Then drain the system and flush it entirely with clean water to eliminate any extra bleach.

Factors to consider before Choosing What to Grow

Virtually any vegetable can be grown hydroponically, but for beginners, it's best to begin small. The very best options are herbs and vegetables that grow quickly, require little maintenance, , and need a wide range of nutrition. Fast-growing plant life are the best, given that they make it easy to evaluate how well one's system works and tweak it as necessary. It's a real letdown to hold back for weeks until harvest time only to discover one's system is not working properly. Maintenance-free vegetation is excellent for beginners because they enable you to concentrate on studying your system-you can move to more technical vegetables later. If you're growing a number of vegetation, additionally, it is crucial to ensure they are similar in their nutritional requirements, for them to grow well collectively.

Lighting

Hydroponic systems tend to be indoor systems situated in places where there is not access to sunlight the whole day. Most edible plants require at least six hours of sunlight every day, with 12 to 16 hours better still. So if you don't have a sunroom or other space with plenty of window exposure, you will likely need to provide supplemental grow lights. Hydroponic kit systems usually include the required light fittings, but if you are piecing together your own components, you'll need to buy individual lighting fixtures.

The best light for a hydroponics system is HID (High-Intensity Density) light fixtures, which range from either HPS (High-Pressure Sodium) or MH (Metallic Halide) bulbs. The light from HPS lights emits a far more orange/red light, which is ideal for vegetation in the vegetative development stage.

T5 is a different type of light found in hydroponic grow rooms. It produces a high-output fluorescent light with low warmth and low energy usage. It is well suited for growing plant cuttings and plant with short development cycles.

Be sure to put your lighting system on a timer to ensure the lights turns on and sets off at exactly the same time each day.

Room Conditions

It is rather important a hydroponic system is established in the right conditions. Important elements include relative humidity, temp, CO_2 levels, and air circulation. The ideal moisture for a hydroponic grow room is from 40 to 60 percent relative humidity. Higher dampness (moisture) levels-especially in rooms with poor air circulation can result in powdery mildew and other fungal problems.

Ideal temperatures are between 68 and 70F. High temperature ranges may cause vegetation to be stunted, and if water temperature gets too high, it may result in root rot.

Your grow room also needs to have enough supply of required amount of CO_2. The ultimate way to ensure this by ensuring the area has a continuous supply of air. More complex hydroponic gardeners may supplement CO_2 levels in the area, because the more CO_2 available, the faster your plant will grow.

Water Quality

Two factors can have an effect on water's ability to provide dissolved nutrition to your plant/vegetation: the amount of mineral salts in water, as measured by PPM; and the pH of water. "Hard" water that contains a higher mineral content won't dissolve nutrition as effectively as water with a lesser mineral content, so you might need to filter system your water if it's high in mineral content. The perfect pH level for water used in a hydroponic system is between 5.8 and 6.2 (slightly acidic). In case your water doesn't meet this level, chemicals may be used to modify the pH into the ideal range.

Nutrients

The nutrients/fertilizers found in hydroponic systems can be purchased in both water and dried forms and in both organic and synthetic types. Either type can be dissolved into drinking water to produce the nutrient mix required by the hydroponic system. The product you use will include both the main macronutrients-nitrogen, potassium, phosphorus, calcium mineral, and magnesium-as well as the key micronutrients, such as trace elements of iron, manganese, boron, zinc, copper, molybdenum, and chlorine.

Many nutrient/fertilizers designed for hydroponic gardening are available, and you ought to have great results if you are using them according to package directions. But stay away from standard garden fertilizers in a hydroponic system, as their formulas are made for use in garden soil, not hydroponic systems.

Choose hydroponic nutritional products that are created for your unique needs. For instance, some are promoted as being suitable for flowering plant, while some are best for promoting vegetative growth, like the greenery of leafy vegetables.

Additional Equipment

Adding to the basic hydroponic set up, it's wise for beginners to purchase a few additional items.

You'll need meters to check the PPM and pH of water, as well as the temperature and relative humidity of the space. There are a combination meters available that will test the pH, PPM, and water temperature. You can even purchase meters that gauge the temperature range and/or the moisture in your grow room.

Based on your climate, you might need a humidifier or dehumidifier to adapt the relative humidity in the develop room for an optimal level.

You might involve some kind of fan or air circulation equipment to enhance the ventilation in your grow room. A simple oscillating fan is effective, but as you get more capable, you might choose a more advanced intake and exhaust system.

Supply of Nutrition to the Plants

In hydroponics, due to the limited nutrient-buffering

capacity of the system and the capability to make fast changes, careful monitoring of the system is necessary. Two aspects of nourishment need to be considered: the supply of nutrients from the nutrient delivery system and the plant nutrient response. For some common crop plants critical levels for some nutrients have been determined.

The rate of recurrence and quantity of the nutritional solution applied depends upon the sort of substrate used (volume and physical-chemical characteristics), the crop (species and stage of development), how big the container is, the type of crop, and irrigation systems used and the prevailing climatic conditions. Plants should be fed daily. The optimum time to manage the nutrient solution is between 6.00 am, and 8.00 am, though water requirements will change considerably during the day, and in one day to the other. The solution is to be applied to the roots, to avoid wetting the leaves to avoid damage and the appearance of diseases. Under no circumstances should plants be permitted to suffer from water stress, as this will affect their final yield. It is recommended that you apply water to the plants once weekly, to be able to flush away any excess salts that have remained. Use double the total amount of water normally applied, but without adding nutrients. about 20 and 50% of the solution is to be drained-off to avoid toxic ions accumulation and an excessive increase in electrical conductivity in the root area of the plant. The surplus nutrient solution drained from containers during daily watering can be reused in the next watering. By the end of the week, this liquid can be discarded.

Desirable pH Selection of Nutrient Solutions

In hydroponic systems, pH is continually changing as the plant grows and develops. pH Changes that is less than 0.1 units doesn't have a significant effect on the plant. So, pH evaluation and control are essential in hydroponic solutions. The optimum pH range for the option of nutrients from most nutrient solutions for some species is 5.5-6.5, but species differ significantly, and many can grow well beyond this range.

Control of Pollutants/Contaminants

Maintaining a sterile root-zone environment is essential to have good plant vigor under soil-less culture. It is challenging to attain and critical to reduce population of plant pathogens in the root zone. Commonly encountered disease in hydroponic solution is wilt, caused by Fusarium and Verticillium. Species of Pythium and Phytophthora destroy basically the primary roots. There is no effective fungicides that can be safely used in hydroponics. Only Metalaxyl has been found highly effective for control of Pythium on vegetable crops, but it is not registered for the utilization. Heat therapy of nutrient solution, in addition, has been found effective in keeping the root-zone free of pathogens. The root death of tomatoes by Pythium was overcome by heating nutrient solutions at 20-22 degree Celsius. In aeroponic system with heated nutrient solution, the roots of ginger plants matured faster and produced slightly higher fresh rhizome yields than plants in the same medium without bottom heat.

List Of Plants that may be grown In Soil-

less/hydroponic Condition

Everything starting from flower to fruit vegetation to medicinal vegetation can be grown using soil-less culture.

Type of plants - Name of the crops

Cereals: Rice (*Oryza sativa*), Maize (*Zea mays*)

Fruits: Strawberry (*Fragaria ananassa*)

Vegetables: Tomato (*Lycopersicon esculentum*), Chilli (*Capsicum frutescens*), Brinjal (*Solanum melongena*), Green bean (*Phaseolus vulgaris*), Beet (*Beta vulgaris*), Winged bean (*Psophocarpus tetragonolobus*), Bell pepper (*Capsicum annum*), Cabbage (*Brassica oleracea var. capitata*), Cauliflower (*Brassica oleracea var. botrytis*), Cucumbers (*Cucumis sativus*), Melons (*Cucumis melo*), Radish (*Raphanus sativus*), Onion (*Allium cepa*)

Leafy vegetables: Lettuce (*Lactuca sativa*), Kang Kong (*Ipomoea aquatica*)

Condiments: Parsley (*Petroselinum crispum*), Mint (*Mentha spicata*), Sweet basil (*Ocimum basilicum*), Oregano (*Origanum vulgare*)

Flower / Ornamental Plants: Marigold (*Tagetes patula*), Roses (*Rosa berberifolia*), Carnations (*Dianthus caryophyllus*), Chrysanthemum (*Chrysanthemum indicum*)

Medicinal crops: Indian Aloe (*Aloe vera*), Coleus (*Solenostemon scutellarioides*)

Fodder plants Sorghum (Sorghum bicolor), Alphalfa (*Medicago sativa*), Barley (*Hordeum vulgare*), Bermuda grass (*Cynodon dactylon*), Carpet grass (*Axonopus compressus*).

These vegetation can be grown on a commercial level using hydroponics/soil-less culture. The application of pesticides is generally prevented under hydroponics system. With minimal pest problems and continuous feeding of nutrition to the roots, efficiency in hydroponics is high, despite limited plant growth due to the reduced amount of carbon dioxide in the atmosphere, or reduced light. To further increase yield, some sealed greenhouses inject carbon-dioxide into their environment to help growth (CO_2 enrichment) or add lights to lengthen the day, control vegetative growth, etc.

Chapter 6

The Future of Hydroponics

Hydroponics can be utilized in underdeveloped countries for food creation in a small space. It really is even feasible to grow hydroponically in regions where there is poor soil conditions, eg. deserts. The desert sand is a good growing medium and seawater may be used to mix nutrient solution after the salts have been removed. The popularity of hydroponics has increased significantly within a brief period of time leading to a rise in experimentation and research in the aspect of indoor and outdoor hydroponic gardening.

Soil vs. Hydroponics

No physiological difference was discovered between plants grown hydroponically and the ones grown on soil. In soil, both inorganic and organic components must be decomposed into inorganic elements before they become available to plants. These elements abide by the particles in the soil and are exchanged in to the garden soil solution where they may be absorbed by plants. In hydroponics, the plant root base are moistened with a nutritional solution comprising the elements. The next processes of nutrient uptake by the plant is the same.

Major Elements, Micronutrient ionic forms mg/L, ppm and concentration range in most nutritional solutions

Concentration RangeElement Ionic Form

Major Elements

Nitrogen (N) NO_3, NH_4 100 to 200

Phosphorus (P) HPO_4 , H_2PO_4 30 to 15

Potassium (K) K^+ 100 to 200

Calcium mineral (Ca) Ca^{2+} 200 to 300

Magnesium element (Mg) Mg^{2+} 30 to 80

Sulfur element (S) SO_4 70 to 150

The Micronutrients, ions and their concentration

Boron (B) BO_3 0.03

Chlorine (Cl) Cl^- -

Copper (Cu) Cu2+ 0.01 to 0.10

Iron (Fe) Fe2+, Fe3+ 2 to 12

Zinc (Zn) Zn2+ 0.05 to 0.50

Manganese (Mn) Mn2+ 0.5 to 2.0

Molybdenum (Mo) Mo04 0.05

Planning Commercial Hydroponics

Hydroponic systems are just one of your options available if you are considering whether to grow a crop. Planning a commercial enterprise should, therefore, follow the standard steps for considering any horticultural business. Do not overlook soil growing. You will need an advantageous reason to employ a hydroponic system rather than soil. If you eventually decided to go with hydroponics, you should measure the benefits and drawbacks of each kind of production system for your crop of choice. For short-term vegetation such as lettuce, the normal choice is recirculating NFT or using flood and drain gravel channels. For long term plants or those very susceptible to root disease, the normal choice is nonrecirculating, media-based systems. Recently, there is an increasing amount of companies supplying a selection of turn-key packages. They sell a complete package of protected structure, hydroponic and support systems, and usually include consulting and marketing agreements.

Hydroponics and Nourishment

There is no conclusive evidence that produce grown hydroponically are more nutritious or healthier than produce grown by some other method, even though some small studies indicate that it might be possible. Some countries, such as Holland, do not differentiate if the produce has been cultivated by hydroponics or by every other method; they only focus on the grade of the produce. Produce quality is much more likely to remain constant in hydroponic systems, as vegetation doesn't through stress like in other systems.

Future Scope Of Hydroponics Technology

Hydroponics is the quickest growing sector of agriculture, and it might flawlessly dominate food production in the future. As human population increases and arable land reduces due to poor management of land, people will turn to new technologies like hydroponics and aeroponics to generate additional channels of crop production. To get a glimpse of this future of hydroponics, we need only to examine some of the early adopters of this technology.

In Tokyo, land is of great value due to the surging population. To feed the citizens of the country while preserving valuable land mass, the United States has considered rice production using hydroponics. The rice will be harvested in underground vaults without making use of soil. Because the surroundings is flawlessly controlled, four cycles of harvest can be performed annually, instead of the traditional single harvest. Hydroponics has also been successfully used in Israel where a dry and arid climate exists. A business called Organitech use hydroponic systems to grow crops in 40-foot (12.19-meter) long shipping containers. They grow berries, citrus fruits, and bananas in large quantities, most of which couldn't normally be grown in Israel's climate. The hydroponics technique produces a high yield of about

One thousand (1,000) times higher than what the same size of land could produce annually. On top of that, the process is totally automated, managed by robots using an assembly line-type system, such as those utilized in manufacturing plants. The shipping containers are then transported throughout the country. There has been a good deal of buzz throughout the scientific community for the potential to use hydroponics in third world countries, where water supplies are limited. Though the initial capital costs of setting up hydroponics systems happens to be a barrier, however in the long-run, as with all technology, costs will decline, making this option a lot more feasible. Hydroponics has got the ability to feed millions in areas of Africa and Asia, where both water and crops are scarce. Hydroponics will also be important to the future of the space program. NASA has considerable hydroponics research plans in position that will benefit current space exploration, as well as future, long-term colonization of Mars or the Moon. Since we haven't yet found soil that can support life in space, and the logistics of transporting soil via the space shuttles seems impractical, hydroponics could be crucial to the future of space exploration.

The advantages of hydroponics in space are two-fold: It provides the potential for a more significant variety of food, and it offers a biological aspect, called a bio-regenerative life support system. This means that as the plants develop, they will absorb carbon-di-oxide and stale air and supply renewed oxygen through the plant's natural growing process. This is important for long-range habitation of both space stations and other planets.

Summary

The hydroponic industry is likely to grow exponentially also in future, as conditions of soil growing is now getting difficult. Especially, in a country like India, where urban concrete conglomerate keeps growing each day, there is certainly no option other than adopting soil-less culture to help enhance the yield and quality of the produce so that we can ensure food security of our country. However, Government intervention and Research Institute having interest it can propel the utilization of the technology.

Chapter 7

Simple DIY Hydroponic Structures that can be built in no time

You really do not need a large garden to grow your fresh produce. Neither do you need many years of experience to create/build your own indoor grow system. This is the beauty of hydroponics.

The entire course is based on flexibility and inventiveness. There are several DIY hydroponics plans all around the World Wide Web.

Below is a collection of the best homemade hydroponics plans you can build. These include plans for beginner, intermediate, and expert level setups.

PVC NFT Hydroponics Program

Large 4" (Four inches) PVC pipes may be used to create your homemade hydroponics system. In this course of action, the plants are positioned in cups that are organized in holders drilled in to the pipes.

The machine is usually watered utilizing a reservoir and pump. It is a closed system, with water moving between pipes and the tank (or reservoir).

This course of action is usually well suited for planting a large amount of small vegetation within a little area. The basic system may house from 20-40 plants.

This technique could be positioned outdoors or indoors. If inside, grow lamps are obviously essential.

The hydroponics technique used in this plant is named NFT. It really is an excellent system for growing vegetation like tomato plants.

Deep water Culture Hydroponics

If you wish to grow plants like tomato and member of the lettuce family indoors, this technique is ideal. Farmers usually use opaque plastic storage box as ideal for the primary nutritional solution container. With regards to the size of the container, from two to eight vegetation could be produced in this technique.

The only additional components needed are a bubbler plus some air hoses to pump in air into the nutritional solution.

The plant could be positioned/placed in net pot, underneath LED grow lamps.

Simple Bucket Hydroponic System

Here is yet a simple hydroponic setup for individuals that are just starting up. All that is needed is a 5-gallon bucket, growing media like coco coir or perlite-vermiculite, and also nutrient mix.

The system works by utilizing the growing media used in the system, to make a capillary action, which moves nutrients up towards the root of the plants.

This system is ideal for people that want to keep things basic; you can also water the system manually. For a system that is automated, you will need another bucket for the reservoir, and a submersible pump, and timer.

Aquarium Hydroponics Raft

This is a very cool task to really get your feet wet in the wonderful world of hydroponics. Additionally, it is a terrific way to make your children connect to the field. As the name suggests, you'll need an aquarium tank to get this to work. This technique may be used to plant small beans or perhaps a single large member of the lettuce family.

Combined with the normal ingredients such as nutritional solution, water, and plants, you'll also need a raft of barge made of foam. The machine can be active or passive, using electric power and pumps.

Drip water Hydroponics

Drip systems could be simple or complicated, based on the needs you have and budget. In a passive system, you can do away with the pumping systems and make use of gravity to bring the nutritional solution to the vegetation.

This will demand some creativity in the placement of your garden and tank/reservoir.

Or you may just make use of a submersible pump and a network of thin tubes to provide the nutrient in small amounts to the plant.

A growing medium is usually preferable for drip systems. Well-known options consist of coir and perlite-vermiculite.

The Passive Bucket Kratky Method

The Kratky unmistakenly one of the easiest hydroponic plans you can start all alone within few hours. This system is excellent for anyone who is just getting started with hydroponics. All you need is a bucket, growing media (such as hydroton, perlite), some net pots, hydroponic nutrients, and pH kits. All these are required to set up a passive system (no electricity required) that can run automatically for weeks without needing maintenance.

You can grow greens like lettuces, spinaches at the beginning or fruit plants like tomatoes after you have gathered enough experience.

Hydroponic Grow Box

This DO-IT-YOURSELF plan is usually an extremely versatile system that may be moved around. It could be made out of any kind of sized storage space tub or bin. It will have a lid.

The machine uses PVC pipes, a submersible pump, and water irrigation sprinkler to provide nutrition and water to the plant.

The plant are housed in net cups filled up with some growth medium. The lid from the box will certainly house the net cups.

Dutch Container Hydroponics

Dutch Buckets are also known as BATO buckets. They are incredibly flexible containers you can use in hydroponics systems of varying complexity.

You can simply have a manual sprinkling system to apply

the nutrient solution many times each day to the plant. Or you may get a basic recirculating system using tubes, pumps, and PVC pipes. To create an automated system, all that is required is usually a simple timer.

This grow system may be used for different sizes of plants. The bigger plants may get a complete bucket, even though several smaller sized herbs could be housed in the same bucket.

With regards to the level of the machine, you can develop a dutch container system in the house, or outside in a greenhouses/patios.

Framework Hydroponic System

The framework hydroponic strategy is nearly the same as the PVC hydroponic program. It uses the same NFT-based concepts to send nutrients and water to the vegetation.

The difference is actually increased verticality. With the addition of new layers of PVC piping at different levels, you are able to grow even more plants in the same space.

The quantity of tubing needed increase, so will the complexity of the pumping system.

This specific system houses the PVC pipes on the wood rack frame. You are able to grow/develop herbs and vegetation such as strawberries and tomato vegetables with this technique.

Vertical Windows Farm

This hydroponic system is a unique idea that solves the issue of light while also creating a remarkable window screen for the outside world.

The program involves using containers to carry plants within a vertical stand setup. Reused water bottles make ideal containers.

A system of tubes/ pipes to take nutrients from your tank towards the plant is essential. Light is provided by natural sunlight. This course of action is perfect for herbs, kale, strawberries, and chard.

Basic Drip Program With Buckets

This is a little more complex than the solitary bucket

program above. It could be cobbled collectively using parts that cost a lower amount than a hundred bucks altogether.

The original plan demands growing 4 plants in separate buckets, all fed by a common tank. This really is an extremely versatile setup that may be extended in Future.

You could change the size of the storage containers, and tank with respect to the size of the plants involved. You could use large 4-gallon buckets or smaller storage containers.

Don't forget to purchase a big tank in the event that you want to include more plants to the setup later on.

Basic Desktop Hydroponic System

The name says everything. This really is an extremely inexpensive hydroponics program that may be positioned on your table.

The program is usually ideal for small plants, just like a herb or lettuce. This is well suited for newbies who don't have much space to grow.

The program entails utilising a half-gallon container or perhaps a coffee can as the primary container. The herb is positioned in a net cup with a growing medium such as Rockwool.

The most expensive aspect of the set up is a small bubbler.

Chapter 8

How to Assemble a Homemade Hydroponic System

Determine the Location of the system

Build the hydroponic system within an enclosed structure, like a greenhouse or the basement of your house, or on a patio or deck located outside. The ground should be level to ensure even coverage of nutrients and water to the vegetation in the system. If placing the system outdoors, protect the system from the elements, such as providing a wind shield/barrier, and check the water levels more regularly due to water reduction from evaporation. During winter or cold temperature, bring the hydroponic system indoors. If putting the system within an interior room of your house, add grow lamps to provide supplemental light to the plant life.

STEP 1

Nutrition makes way through pipes by water push

STEP 1

Assemble the Hydroponic System

The system includes six growing tubes made from 6" PVC pipe, a stand and trellis manufactured from PVC, a 50-gallon nutrient tank, a pump, and a manifold. The container rests under the desk of 6" PVC growing pipes, and the pump rests inside the tank to push nutrition up to the vegetation with a manifold of smaller PVC pipes and plastic pipes. Each growing pipe has a drainpipe leading back again to the tank. The manifold rests on the top of the pipes and sends pressurized water to the pipes. To make the nutrition get to the plant in this technique, water is forced through a square of PVC, the manifold, and then gets shot out to small plastic material pipes that run inside each one of the larger growing pipes. The nutrient pipes have really small openings in them, one opening between each plant site. The nutrition shoots out the opening and spray the plant roots with nutrients. At exactly the same time, the water makes air bubbles, therefore, the vegetation gets enough oxygen.

STEP 2

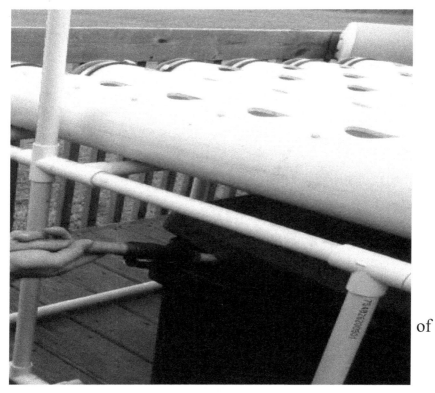

of

Mix the Nutrition and Drinking water in the Tank

Fill up the 50-gallon reservoir with water. Then add two cups of nutrition to the tank (or as suggested by the fertilizer label), start the pump, and allow system run for approximately thirty minutes to get all the nutrients thoroughly mixed.

STEP 3

Among the easiest ways to plant a hydroponic garden is by using purchased seedlings, particularly if you do not have time to grow the seeds yourself. The main element is to find the healthiest plant you will get and then remove every of the soil off their root base. To clean the soil from the roots, submerge the root ball in a bucket of lukewarm to cold water (image 1). Water that's too warm or too chilly can send the vegetable into shock. Softly separate the root base to get all the soil out. Any garden soil remaining on the roots could clog in the tiny spray openings in the nutrient pipes.

After the root is clean, pull as much root base as possible underneath the planting cup and then add extended clay pebbles to hold the plant and set it upright (Image 2). The extended clay pebbles are hard, but they're also very light so that they don't harm the plant roots.

STEP 4

STEP 4

Tie the Plant to the Trellis

With the use of plant clips and string, connect the plant to the trellis. The string gives them support to climb upward directly, which really helps to maximize the limited space in the small area. Loosely connect the string to the top of the trellis (Image 1), the clips and string are to be attached to the bottom of each plant (Image 2), and softly wind the tips of the plant around the string.

STEP 5

Switch on the Pump and Monitor the System Daily

Check the water levels daily; in a few regions, it might be essential to check it twice each day, depending on water loss credited to excess heat and evaporation. Check the pH and nutrient levels every couple of days. Since the pump works full time, a timer is not necessary, but make sure the tank doesn't dry up, or the pump will burn.

STEP 6

Monitor Vegetation Growth

A couple of weeks after planting, the plants will completely cover the trellis because they'll have all water and nutritional requirements they need to develop rapidly. It is critical to keep a detailed eye on vegetation growth and clip and tie the plant stalks every couple of days.

STEP 7

Look for indicators of pests and diseases

Inspect for Pests and Diseases

Look for indications of pests and diseases, like the existence of insect pest, bugs, chewed leaves and foliar diseases. One diseased vegetable can quickly infect others since they are so near to one another. Remove any sick plant you notice immediately. Because plant grown hydroponically need not spend their energy looking for food, they can spend additional time growing. This can help these to be healthier and stronger because they can use a few of that energy to battle off diseases. Because the leaves of the vegetation never get damp unless it rains, they're significantly less likely to get leaf fungi, mold, and mildew.

Despite the fact that hydroponic vegetation are proficient

at overcoming diseases, they still have to combat pests. Even though it's hydroponic, bugs and caterpillars can nevertheless discover a way into the garden. Pick off and get rid of any insects/bugs you see.

Making Hydroponic Solution at home

- Purchase the nutrients. You should purchase Nitrogen, Phosphorus, Calcium, etc. to help make the base of your fertilizer.

- Use clean water. You should make use of filtered water.

- Mix the salts with the water. You should add the salts slowly into the water.

- Add micronutrients.

- Adjust the EC level.

- Adjust the pH level.

CPSIA information can be obtained
at www.ICGtesting.com
Printed in the USA
BVHW011450110121
597542BV00007B/572